ENGINEERED BY NATURE

CAVE OF CRYSTALS

BY MARTHA LONDON

CONTENT CONSULTANT
ERIC FRITZ
GEM AND MINERAL MUSEUM MANAGER
UNIVERSITY OF ARIZONA

Kids Core
An Imprint of Abdo Publishing
abdobooks.com

abdobooks.com

Published by Abdo Publishing, a division of ABDO, PO Box 398166, Minneapolis, Minnesota 55439. Copyright © 2021 by Abdo Consulting Group, Inc. International copyrights reserved in all countries. No part of this book may be reproduced in any form without written permission from the publisher. Kids Core™ is a trademark and logo of Abdo Publishing.

Printed in the United States of America, North Mankato, Minnesota
022020
092020

Cover Photo: Javier Trueba/MSF/Science Source
Interior Photos: Carsten Peter/National Geographic/Christie's Images/Xinhua News Agency/Newscom, 4–5; Carsten Peter/Speleoresearch & Films/National Geographic, 7, 21, 22, 24; iStockphoto, 8 (left), 8 (right), 12–13; Javier Trueba/MSF/Science Source, 10, 16, 18–19, 25, 26, 28; Joel Arem/Science Source, 15; Rainer Lesniewski/iStockphoto, 28–29

Editor: Marie Pearson
Series Designer: Megan Ellis

Library of Congress Control Number: 2019917964

Publisher's Cataloging-in-Publication Data

Names: London, Martha, author.
Title: Cave of Crystals / by Martha London
Description: Minneapolis, Minnesota : Abdo Publishing, 2021 | Series: Engineered by nature | Includes online resources and index.
Identifiers: ISBN 9781532192845 (lib. bdg.) | ISBN 9781098210748 (ebook)
Subjects: LCSH: Crystals, Cave of (Mexico)--Juvenile literature. | Natural monuments--Juvenile literature. | Caves--Juvenile literature. | National parks and reserves--Juvenile literature. | Landforms--Juvenile literature.

CONTENTS

The crystals look huge next to humans.

CHAPTER 1

CRYSTAL TOWERS

Scientists step into the Cave of Crystals. Huge columns of white crystals surround the scientists. Some crystals are 36 feet (11 m) tall. The columns are as thick as tree trunks. Scientists estimate the largest crystals weigh more than 60 tons (55 metric tons).

The crystals gleam as the scientists shine their flashlights. The scientists wear orange suits filled with ice packs. The scientists are sweaty. The Cave of Crystals is nearly 140 degrees Fahrenheit (60°C). Oxygen masks wheeze. It is hard to breathe in the heat. The scientists have 30 minutes to gather as much information as possible. After that, they will need to leave the cave to cool down.

Discovery Under a Mountain

The Cave of Crystals is in the state of Chihuahua in Mexico. It lies under the Sierra de Naica mountain in the town of Naica.

Scientists needed special gear to keep them cool and help them breathe in the cave.

How Deep Is 1,000 Feet?

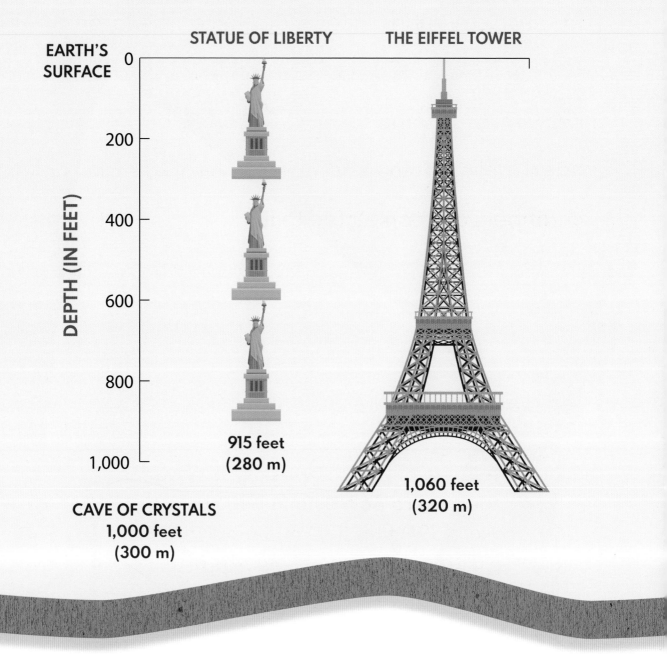

EARTH'S SURFACE

STATUE OF LIBERTY

THE EIFFEL TOWER

DEPTH (IN FEET)

0

200

400

600

800

1,000

915 feet
(280 m)

1,060 feet
(320 m)

CAVE OF CRYSTALS
1,000 feet
(300 m)

The Cave of Crystals is 1,000 feet (300 m) underground. That is deeper than three Statues of Liberty are tall. The Eiffel Tower is a little taller than the cave is deep.

There are several connected caves with large crystals under Sierra de Naica. The largest **chamber** is the Cave of Crystals. It is 1,000 feet (300 m) below the surface. The Cave of Crystals has a large, central chamber. Several smaller chambers are connected to it.

Cave of Swords

The Cave of Swords was discovered under Sierra de Naica in 1910. The cave is 390 feet (120 m) below the mountain. The Cave of Swords also has large crystals. But they are smaller than those in the Cave of Crystals.

Scientists studied the crystals to learn how they had formed.

Crystals have flat sides. The crystals in the Cave of Crystals are made out of a **mineral** called selenite. Selenite is white or clear. Selenite crystals have four or six sides. The Cave of Crystals formed over thousands of years. But scientists didn't know it existed until 2000.

Explore Online

Look at the website below. Does it give any new information related to Chapter One?

Crystal Caves

abdocorelibrary.com/cave-of-crystals

Magma sometimes reaches
Earth's surface. Then it is
called lava.

CHAPTER 2

FORMED IN HEAT AND WATER

The Cave of Crystals needed heat, water, and minerals to form. About 26 million years ago, **magma** flowed up through cracks in Earth's crust. Magma is hot liquid rock. Magma filled a hollow chamber deep below the base of Sierra de Naica.

The magma heated water in the ground above it. As the water heated up, it expanded. It rose through cracks in the ground. The soil in the ground contained minerals. When the water rose through the ground, the minerals **dissolved** in the water. They traveled with the water. Eventually the water filled the caves beneath Sierra de Naica.

Other Chambers

The Cave of Crystals is made up of several connected chambers. All of the chambers have crystals. But not all of the crystals are shaped the same. Some look like cauliflower. Others look like thread. Crystals form many shapes.

The selenite crystals in the cave started small.

Crystallizing

The water was hot. This heat stopped the minerals from forming crystals. But over time, the water cooled to just below 136 degrees Fahrenheit (58°C). The water temperature then stayed consistent. Selenite **crystallizes** at these temperatures. Tiny pieces of selenite in the water attached together. As the selenite continued to build, small crystal towers began to form.

It took hundreds of thousands of years for some of the crystals to reach their huge size.

As long as mineral-rich water was in the cave, the crystals continued to grow. But it took a long time for the largest towers to form. The oldest crystals are at least 500,000 years old.

John Rakovan studies crystals. He explained why the Cave of Crystals is unique:

> When crystals get larger and larger, they become less [like crystals in appearance], typically. . . . Scientists didn't think it was possible to get large crystals that are so . . . perfect [in shape].

Source: Ker Than. "Giant Crystal Caves." *National Geographic*, 8 Oct. 2010, nationalgeographic.com. Accessed 29 Oct. 2019.

What's the Big Idea?

Read this quote carefully. What is its main idea? Explain how the main idea is supported by details.

The mining company Peñoles
ran the Sierra de Naica mine.

CHAPTER 3

STUDYING THE CAVES

Sierra de Naica has resources that people mine. A mining company built tunnels in the mountain that connected with the caves. Many of the caves in the mountain were filled with water.

The mining company pumped water out of the Cave of Crystals in 2000. Two miners discovered the crystals once the water was gone. Selenite is fragile. A fingernail can scratch the crystals. The smaller crystals crack easily.

The mining company put a door over the cave entrance. Only scientists could enter the cave. This protected the cave and crystals. It also protected people. Without proper gear, the heat and humidity in the cave can be deadly.

Scientists studied the crystals. Some scientists believed tiny **organisms** could live in the cave. In 2008 and 2009, they took samples from the crystals.

Scientists prepare to enter the door to the Cave of Crystals, *right*.

Scientists collected liquid from the crystals.

Small amounts of liquid are trapped in the crystals. Scientists took some of that liquid. They studied the samples. There were tiny organisms in the liquid. The creatures were too small to see with the human eye. Scientists continued to study the ancient organisms. Scientists were able to grow more of them.

Life in Extreme Places

Some of the tiny organisms from the Cave of Crystals were more than 10,000 years old. The organisms help scientists understand the places life can exist on Earth. Scientists use this information when they study other planets. Scientists make predictions about where life might exist in space.

The crystals in the caves come in many shapes and sizes.

Flooded Caves

In 2015, the mining company left Sierra de Naica. Two years later, the company stopped pumping water from the Cave of Crystals. Groundwater is slowly filling the chambers again. People cannot get into the caves anymore.

The crystals in the Cave of Crystals are the largest
ever found.

The crystals could not grow while the cave was pumped dry.

Scientists are disappointed they cannot continue to study this amazing location. However, scientists also believe the caves are healthier when they are filled with water. The crystals are fragile. Air makes them even more fragile. Without the mineral water, the crystals are not stable. Air makes the crystals break down. Allowing the caves to flood means it is possible the crystals will continue to grow for many more thousands of years.

Explore Online

Visit the website below. Did you learn any new information about tiny organisms that wasn't in Chapter Three?

Extremophiles

abdocorelibrary.com/cave-of-crystals

MAP

SONORA

CHIHUAHUA

NAICA

COAHUILA

MEXICO

DURANGO

ZACATECAS

CAVE OF CRYSTALS

NAYARIT

UNITED STATES
OF AMERICA

Gulf of Mexico

NUEVO
LEÓN

TAMAULIPAS

SAN LUIS POTOSÍ

- The Cave of Crystals is in the town Naica.

- The crystals are made of selenite.

- A mining company pumped the cave dry between 2000 and 2017. Scientists studied it during this period.

Glossary

chamber
a hollow portion of an area or object

crystallizes
comes together to form a solid

dissolved
became part of a liquid

magma
liquid rock

mineral
a material from the ground that has never been alive

organisms
living things

Online Resources

To learn more about the Cave of Crystals, visit our free resource websites below.

Visit **abdocorelibrary.com** or scan this QR code for free Common Core resources for teachers and students, including vetted activities, multimedia, and booklinks, for deeper subject comprehension.

Visit **abdobooklinks.com** or scan this QR code for free additional online weblinks for further learning. These links are routinely monitored and updated to provide the most current information available.

Learn More

Dennie, Devin. *My Book of Rocks and Minerals*. DK, 2017.

Honovich, Nancy. *Rocks and Minerals*. National Geographic, 2016.

Index

About the Author

Martha London writes books for young readers full-time. When she isn't writing, you can find her hiking in the woods.